YVONNE PORCELLA

A COLORFUL BOOK

Produced by
Roderick Kiracofe

YVONNE PORCELLA

A COLORFUL BOOK

Published in the United States by C&T Publishing, Martinez, California.
ISBN 0-914881-81-7
Library of Congress Catalog Card Number: 85-90510

Third Printing, 1993

Printed by Nissha Printing Company, Ltd., Kyoto, Japan.
Color separations by the printer.
Book production and print supervision by Roderick Kiracofe,
San Francisco.
Typographical composition in Gill Sans and Weiss by Rock & Jones,
Oakland, California.
Book design by Roderick Kiracofe and Jeanne Jambu, San Francisco.
Editing by Harold Nadel, San Francisco.
Photography by Sharon Risedorph, San Francisco.
Photographs on pages 18, 19, 20, 24, 26, 45, 61, 65, 66, 85 (top),
87 (right), 88, 89 by Elaine Faris Keenan, San Francisco.

Cover (front and back): details of *Pasha on the 10:04*, kimono, 1984.

For information on fabric painting, clothing classes,
workshops, and lectures contact:
Porcella Studios
3619 Shoemake Avenue
Modesto, California 95351
209/524-1134

ACKNOWLEDGMENTS

Every book comes together with behind-the-scenes help from family and friends. I would like to thank my husband, Bob, for accepting my art and supporting my projects; our sons, Steve, Greg and Don, for listening to me expound on how great life is; our daughter Suzanne and her husband Tim for always being home when the traveling grandma comes through town; and Nick, Vince and Eric for liking my quilts. A special thank you to good friends Maggie Brosnan and Steve Kalar, who always help above and beyond. I would also like to thank Jean Ray Laury, Janice Rhea, Sonya Lee Barrington, Elaine Faris Keenan, Sharon Risedorph, Jeanne Jambu, Harold Nadel, my sister Marilou Locey, all of whom helped with their special talents. I am most grateful to Roderick Kiracofe, who helped pull this book together and guide it to completion.

CONTENTS

Foreword 9

Introduction 11

Yvonne Porcella:
A Colorful Book 16

Fabric Painting Techniques 106

An Easy Approach to
Fabric Piecing 112

List of Color Plates 116

Bibliography 118

Source List 119

FOREWORD

Most artists are recognized by their styles. We can identify their works anywhere. We know, without looking for identification, when we see a quilt by Jan Myers, or Sonya Lee Barrington, or Michael James.

We also know when we see a quilt of Yvonne Porcella's. Color saturates her style so thoroughly that perhaps we identify her work more through color than any other single aspect of design.

"Intrepid" is the word that, for me, best describes Yvonne's approach. She is fearless. There is no timidity in her work. Her combinations are exuberant and energetic. A visual review of her work makes it obvious that she adheres to no set rules or theories: she is not confined by what someone may have decreed is a "good" color combination. Combining colors that sometimes startle us into new ways of seeing, she works from an apparently limitless palette. She has no "set" combinations, and yet it is her special and unique way of combining colors that creates the dazzling effects. Whether dramatic, dynamic, delicate or subtle (or several of these simultaneously), we know that here is a colorist who recognizes no arbitrary or academic limitations on her choices.

Yvonne's grasp of color was evident in her early weaving. When I first met her (at a weaver's conference), it was like finding a kindred soul, someone who loved color and embraced it joyously. She wore it and used it with imagination and zest. No color was ever allowed to be lazy: each was required to do its full share, to function completely. No color was just "there" as a passive element; it was there because it was working.

The art of weaving seems to me to be most like painting—threads of color mix, like the dots of the pointillist paintings or the strokes of color in the impressionists' works. Depth and richness grow out of combinations of interacting colors. A red composed of five variations of red contains an impact of color that is more vibrant, alive and rich than any single red can be.

Yvonne's background in weaving seems to have influenced the color choices in her present work. The impact of her color creates excitement, visually and emotionally. Just when we think our rods and cones verge on overstimulation, they encounter repose. The contrast refreshes. It is this ability to move from one effect to another to create responses that run the gamut from peaceful to explosive that most typifies Yvonne's work. She helps us all experience the overwhelming brilliance and power of color.

—Jean Ray Laury

INTRODUCTION

When I am teaching, the most frequent questions I am asked are "How do you begin your designs for a quilt or garment?" or "Where do you get your ideas?" or "How do you know which colors to put together?" This book will attempt to answer these questions.

In 1962, I began to explore the world of fiber art as a beginning weaver. I wanted to make my own fabric so I could sew a one-of-a-kind garment. My thought was that if I created the fabric, no one else in the world would have an outfit like mine. At that time I knew nothing of color or fiber or weaving. Little by little, I learned the art of weaving, the mechanics of the loom and how to make a successful fabric. I must admit my first attempt was less than perfect, because I did not know the mechanics of color. I learned by trial and error. As I began to look around me, I found other handwoven fabrics that I liked: I began to examine the sources of their appeal. I explored the color combinations of threads and pattern weaves. It was at this time that I began to collect textiles from other cultures. Textile collecting led me to an interest in how garments were made from handwoven fabrics. So began a modest collection of folk costumes. The folk garments educated me in basic garment construction. I believe my current expertise in garments and quiltmaking stems from these early interests in fabrics and costumes.

There are many areas of the world with textiles and garments that are particularly interesting to me. Inspiration comes from these different cultures. It is hard to say which I like best, but Japanese textiles, as well as those from Afghanistan and the Russian steppes, make up a large part of my collection.

In 1974 I got a room of my own, a work space for my exclusive use. That meant I would no longer sew standing up at the laundry counter or use the dining-room table to cut out fabric. My family has been very supportive of my work; therefore, I wanted a studio in my home, so that I could be creative but still be a part of family activities. My studio is a large room upstairs, over the family room. Entry is by a spiral stairway from the kitchen. It is definitely MY room, and I have filled it with paraphernalia that inspire me. Having my own work space has allowed me the freedom to be creative and to grow as an artist.

My ideas for garments or quilts appear to flow from some nebulous place. But on close examination my inspirations can be traced to those objects which I have collected, those which fill my studio and my home. When putting together this book, I assembled many of the items that have influenced my work. These are set up in composite photographs so the viewer can trace the origin of an idea.

Along with ethnic textiles and garments, I have managed to add a few old quilts to my collection. How do I select them? I do gravitate toward quilts with a one-inch postage stamp patchwork design, such as nine patch. If the price is within my budget, or the quilt has prairie points around the edge, or the quilt needs a good home, I need it. It is also likely to find its way into my collection if the quilt is unusual silk patchwork or double-sided, with patchwork designs on either front or back. In other words, although I know I should have certain rules for buying old quilts, I often can't resist a particular quilt and have to find a reason for adding it to my collection.

I have a wonderful old silk quilt which was featured in *The Quilt Digest* 2 (1984). It is referred to as *Victorian silk work*. Louise Townsend in *Quilter's Newsletter Magazine*, issue 161 (April 1984), said in her book review: "I felt that he [Rod Kiracofe] was pushing the limits of my tolerance for the definition of a quilt—only to turn another page and find the most incredible Victorian silk work quilt I had ever seen. It was a hundred years old, yet it looked so different from the traditional idea of a quilt design that once again I had to admit that there are many ways to define the word *quilt*—and not all of them are new." When I saw this quilt I, too, was fascinated by the quiltmaker's choice of bits or snips of silk to make a quilt. I have used this Victorian quilt as inspiration for my "Diamonds on Ice" and "Firebird" kimonos.

As a fabric user, I am always looking for something new. I no longer weave my own fabrics, but I still like to try different materials. When the metallic fabrics appeared, I chose to try the woven fabric instead of the bonded metallic surface on tricot. The woven fabric maintains an integrity with my weaving background. I have a section in this book of opulent designs which includes work with metallic fabrics used along with traditional cottons and silks. In this section I also included rhinestones and sequins attached to garments, to add to the glitter.

I enjoy traditional Japanese art and textiles. My favorite book is *The Tale of Genji* by Murasaki Shikibu, written in the eleventh century. I like to open this book at random and read from the many color-inspiring passages. I also enjoy the genre and *ukiyo-e* paintings and from them gain inspiration for my pastel painted works. I also favor the Japanese contemporary color ethic of combining conflicting colors or striking contrasts.

Along with collecting material possessions, I also treasure friendships of other artists and study the work of some of the world's best-known artists. I have a friend— Pink by name—who fills me with inspiration. Whenever we meet, the creative energy flows. We write letters, and the postman wonders. I must admit that Pink is more outlandish in her stationery and lack of respect for postal traditions than I. She calls me Magenta or sometimes addresses letters to Señorita Magenta or Lady Magenta and I sign my letters "Love, Magenta." A composite in the book is dedicated to Pink—all the kitsch she collects, decorates her letters with and gives as small presents. When looking at Pink's art, one really has to note every minute detail.

When I began to use many bright colors in clothing, I also included black and white. This was to give the eye a place to rest. I love the use of black and white in textiles in my collection. Black and white still appear together frequently in my designs, although I don't have any fixed rules about using them.

I have found myself working with certain color combinations during various times of my life. As a weaver I had my red period, when I wove everything to co-ordinate with a particular red dress. This was followed by a lengthy rainbow period. I believe I am still involved with rainbows, and I still find it difficult to escape red. I enjoy using rainbow colors in my work even if the piece is basically black and white. The rainbow colors add life.

A favorite time of the year is February, because it gives us Valentine's Day. Red is the color I use often, and I have chosen to end the main section of this book with a composite picture of hearts with works in red.

I began painting silk fabrics for use in quilts and garments because I wanted an alternative to dyeing fabrics with synthetic dyestuffs. I wanted an easier way to color fabric quickly. When selecting fabric for painting, I paint on anything that is white, be it cotton, silk or wool.

When I begin a piece, I start with color, picking and harmonizing fabrics to express a bold or soft statement. *Red/magenta/purple/chartreuse/orange/yellow/turquoise/aubergine* are the sounds of colors. Just saying the words conjures up the vivid impressions of colors—fabrics—I might use in a quilt or garment. For me each color has a feeling associated with it, and I use color to express my sentiments in a piece. If I use silk fabrics which I will paint, I want soft colors that capture the feel of the silk, the luminous quality that some silk fabrics seem to have. I use peach, lavender, pink, sea-foam green, mauve, pale yellow. If I want a bold statement, I choose vivid colors: red, yellow and green; magenta, orange and turquoise; blue, purple and orange; purple, red and green. I work from an intuitive understanding of color. I believe my color sense comes from everything I have ever seen or experienced during my life. I am not fluent in the academic terminology of hue or chroma. I have not had formal art or color training; my college degree is in nursing. However, as I work more with color, I find it necessary to educate myself in some of the rules and terminology. To be a serious artist, I tell myself that one should take advantage of the theories of color and learn as much as possible. There are many people who have devoted their lives to exploring the properties of color. I find it interesting to study what they have discovered about the intricate subject of color.

Color physics appears complex because it deals with the dispersion of light into colors of the spectrum and light waves. A good understanding of color used in fabric arts can be learned without all this complexity. Colors can cause an emotional response, and this study is the psychology of color. If you ever wonder why some advertising companies choose certain colors for a business logo, they do so because, in each society, there are certain colors which evoke certain responses. Red, for instance, is the color of fire and blood, magic and sorcery. It is the most sensual, and it is the symbol of life. Red attracts attention. It is used to make us STOP. Blue is the color of the sky and the ocean. Blue is the maternal color. Blue is cool and restful. Green is the color of living things. It is eternal life. It is also the color to make us GO.

For the fabric artist, it is necessary to understand some of the basics of color theory and then experiment with the medium chosen—fabric. I think it is important to have a working knowledge of primary, secondary, and tertiary colors, warm and cool, tints and shades, complements, harmonies, contrasts and value. The simplest way to begin is to purchase a color wheel from a local art-supply store. Study the wheel and all of its combinations. I have found it valuable to actually paint color exercises. It is the physical process of mixing colors to match the color wheel that educates us about the actual components of each individual color. I used textile paint on white cotton fabric to make a notebook of exercises. If nothing else, one learns that red, yellow, and blue pigments can be used to make most other colors. Red, yellow, and blue are considered the primary colors by the majority of colorists.

This book does not pretend to cover color theory. There are books by masters whose work on color is recognized as authority. The purpose of this book is for you to enjoy looking at my personal expressions of color. I have divided the book into groupings of some of my favorite color combinations. The informational section of this book includes fabric painting and some of the techniques for achieving interesting surface designs. Also included are simple strip-piecing techniques that I use to design garments or quilts.

This book is—my work, my inspirations, my colors.

—Yvonne Porcella

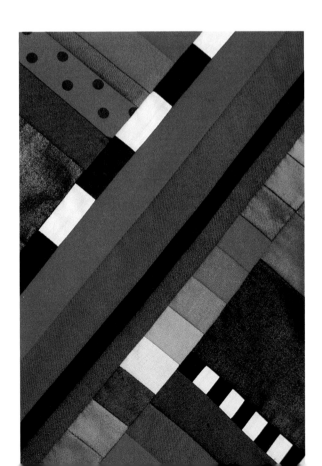

"Red and orange, green and blue, shiny yellow, purple too. All the colors that you know are found up in the rainbow."

—Thom Klika

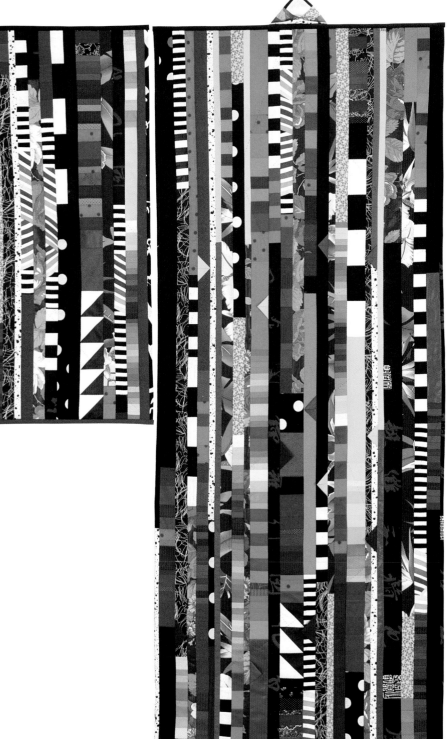

"At the end of 1981 I visited the Canadian Rockies
and again watched the beauty of the sinking sun as it laid
various colors on my heart."
— Itchiku Kubota

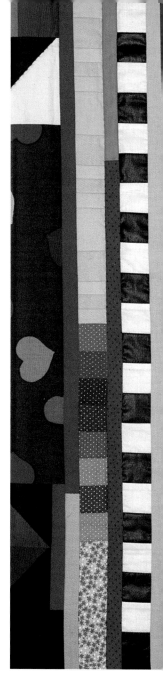

"Color occasionally just takes charge. The more I work with it, the less I seem to know about it and the more I trust it."

—Anne Truitt

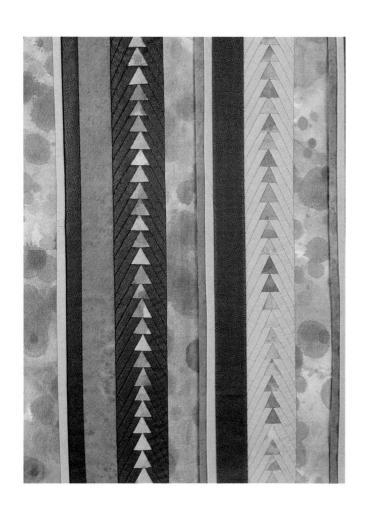

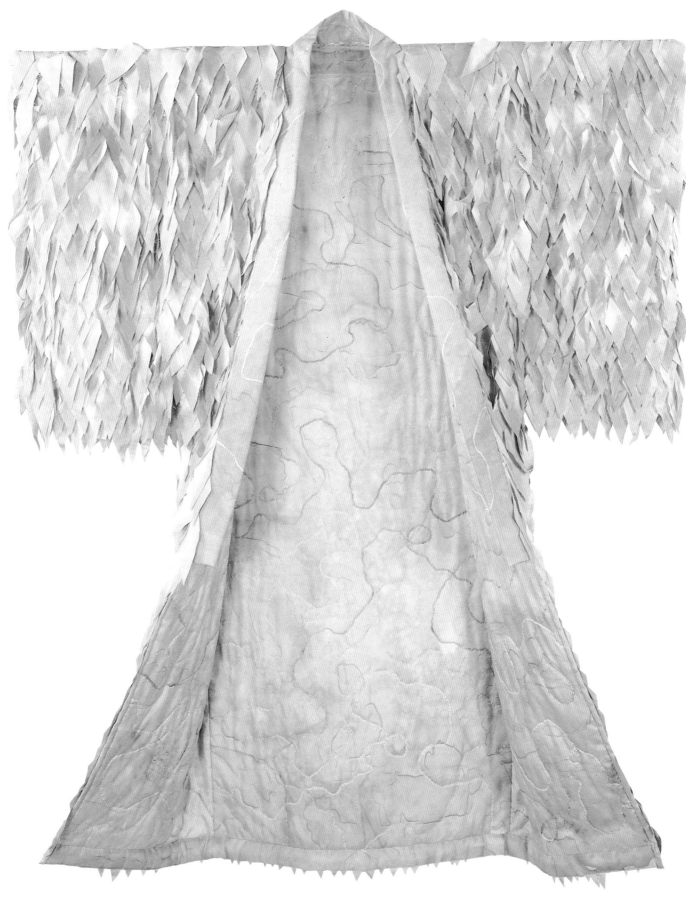

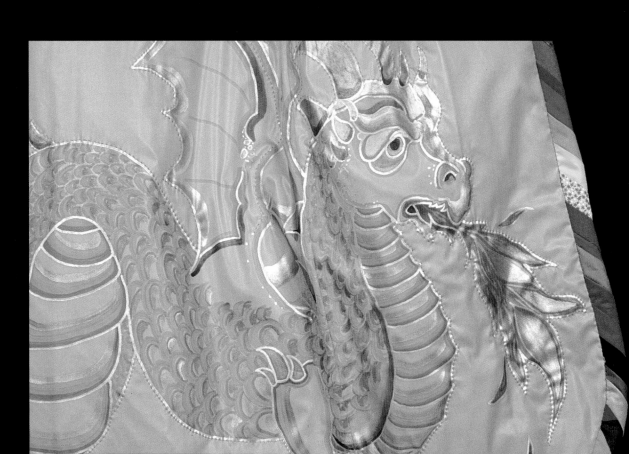

"Red is the great clarifier—bright, cleansing, and revealing. It makes all other colors beautiful. I can't imagine becoming bored with red—it would be like becoming bored with the person you love."
                                                                    —Diana Vreeland

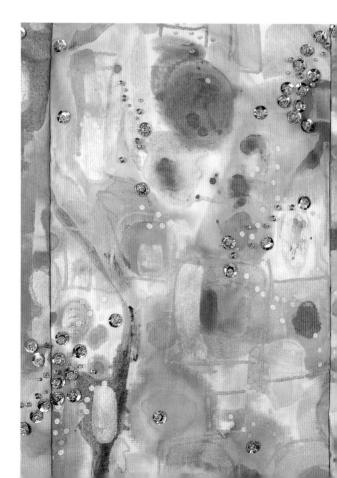

"I never start out only with color. I start out as a spacemaker on a flat thing with four corners. But color is the first message on the picture plane."
—Helen Frankenthaler

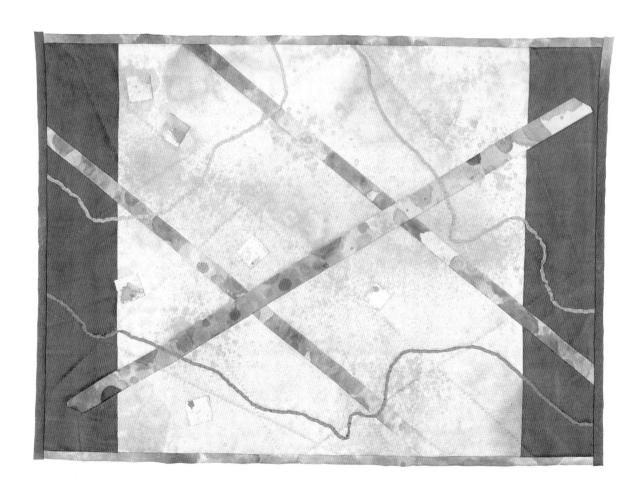

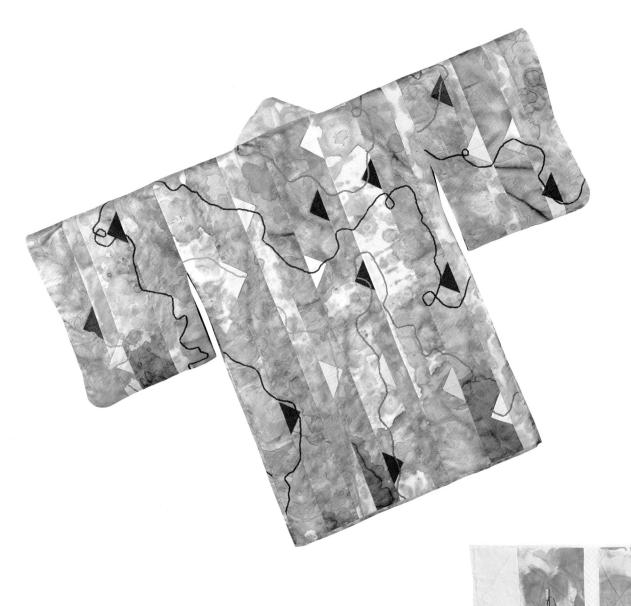

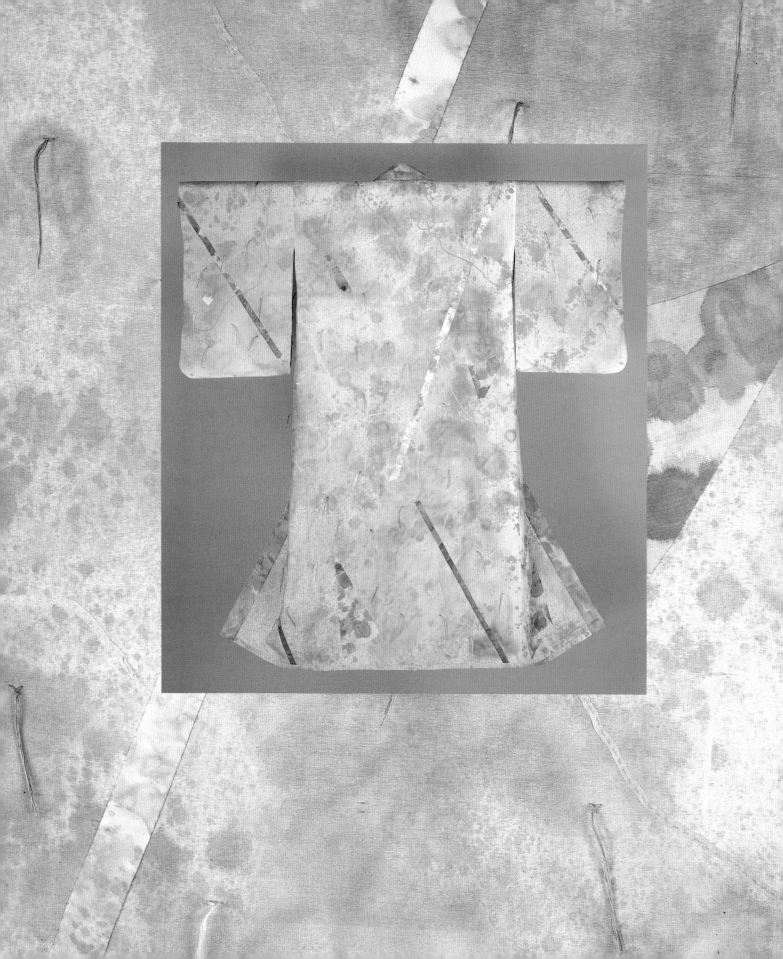

"I broke a piece off an anthill in Uganda and brought it home. The result is a positively magic shade of brown."

—Hundertwasser

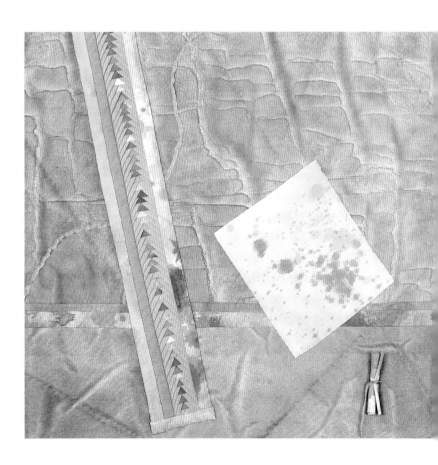

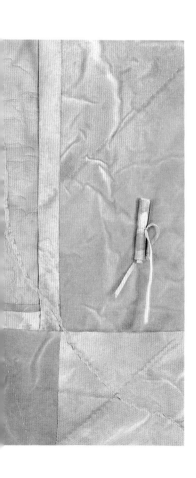

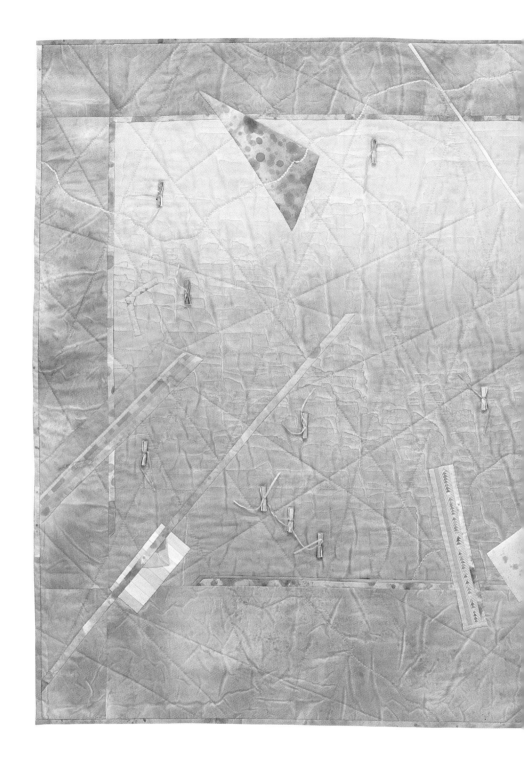

"Her messenger was a rather tall girl in a singlet of a deep purple, a robe of lilac lined with blue, and a gossamer cloak of saffron."
—Lady Murasaki

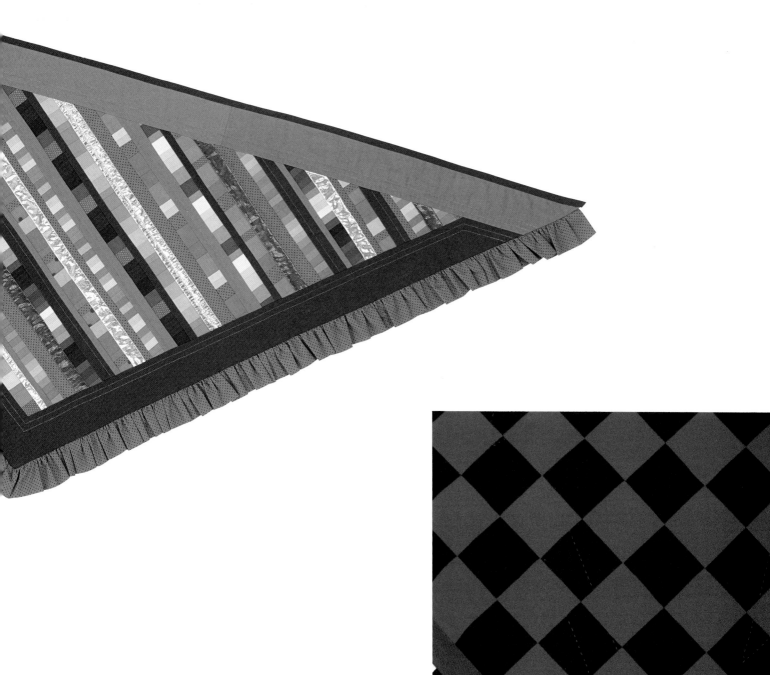

"Seeing is an indirect process. 'Color' originates as a sensation."
—Harald Kueppers

"If the Rainbow came each day do you suppose we'd care?
Perhaps we find it beautiful because it is so rare!"
— Thom Klika

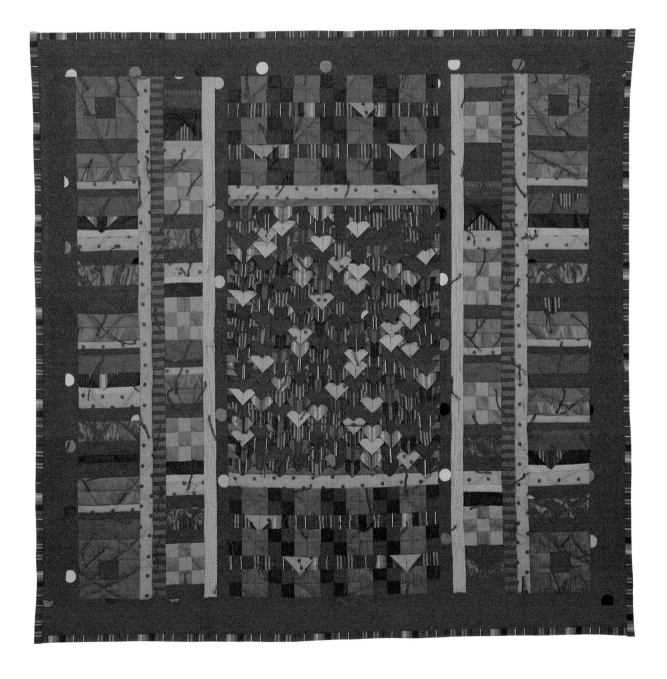

"... and along the galleries wisteria was beginning to send forth its lavender."
—Lady Murasaki

FABRIC PAINTING TECHNIQUES

Dyeing is a common term used to describe the coloring of fabric. The subject is vast, as are the products available. Products are available for different fabrics and effects, and each has special advantages. For the beginning student, experimentation can be costly, due to the price of fabric and supplies. A good book on the subject helps define the various categories: I recommend *Surface Design for Fabric* by Richard M. Proctor and Jennifer F. Lew.

To simplify the subject, I must distinguish between dyes and pigments. Dye is usually synthetic and bonds chemically with the fiber. It can be purchased as powder or liquid and usually requires a chemical fixative or steam to make the fabric colorfast. Dye can be painted directly on fabric or used in a dyebath into which the fabric is submerged. Textile pigment or ink only coats the surface fibers; it is water-soluble and is set by ironing. Pigment may be painted, stamped, silk-screened, or stenciled on fabric. I have experimented with both dye and pigment and, in this book, have concentrated on fabric painting with pigment. This is the easy and inexpensive way to begin coloring fabric. The tools are easy to find and the techniques simple and quick.

There are many products available; the labels will state which fabric types they are suitable for. Natural-fiber fabrics will generally accept the textile pigments. If the fabric is synthetic, it may be necessary to add a binder to the product, and the binder may stiffen the fabric. I prefer working with pure cotton or silk, especially silk fabric that is easy to tear so I can use my painted fabric in strip piecing. I use silk twill, which is bleached white and tears into a strip of even width. I also use silk pongee (un-bleached), silk noil, and China silk.

When I paint fabric using textile pigment, I add a sufficient amount of water to dilute the colors for a soft pastel result. I am careful not to use excessive pigment, which will stiffen the fabric. I suggest using a fiber-reactive dye for dark, intense colors, rather than building up paint onto the surface of the fabric in an attempt to get dark colors with textile pigment. Although I have tested many different brands, I do not recommend one over the other. It is best for you to determine which is best for your needs.

To begin, I suggest limiting the colors and experimenting with color mixing. This eliminates the added expense of buying too many colors and allows you to test the particular product. Red, yellow and blue should give you the basics and, in a good product, will produce many colors by mixing. You could add green and magenta to the basic three colors.

Be sure to wear old clothes or an apron when painting. Cover the work space with plastic. (Please note that an embossed plastic drop cloth, while easy to handle, may leave the embossed image on your fabric.) It is best to use a smooth plastic surface under your fabric. Always protect your iron by using a press cloth over wet paint. You can iron directly if the paint is absolutely dry. Some pigments will permanently color fabric even without the required heat setting. See individual product labels for the required time for heat setting, as well as any special instructions.

SOME HINTS FOR SEWING WITH SILK

1. I generally do not pre-wash silk before painting if I will be wetting the entire piece with water and paint in the coloring process. However, if there is sizing or a permanent-press finish on the silk, it may be necessary to pre-wash to remove these finishes. Each fabric type presents its own particular set of requirements.

2. Painted silk is hand-washable after painting. Some pigments leave a residual odor on the fabric, so washing is necessary after heat-setting to remove the odor. Individual painted fabrics should be tested for dry cleaning; see product information.

3. Silk will tear and ravel a few threads on each side of the tear. Silks will ravel two or three threads, depending on the weight of the silk. Silk tears only from selvage to selvage (weft direction). Clip the selvage edge about one inch and tear across the fabric to the opposite selvage. Some silk weaves will tear in the other direction (with the warp) but fracture the torn edge so much that the fabric is distorted beyond ¼".

4. Silk can be sewn with any sewing thread. It is not necessary to use silk thread.

5. Press the fabric with a steam iron after sewing each seam.

TOOLS AND SUPPLIES

Iron and press cloth
Disposable aluminum pie tins
1" nylon paint brush (hardware store)
4" natural bristle brush (hardware store)
Artist's acrylic paint brush — round #6
Plastic plumbing pipe or acrylic clear tube—
    1" diameter by 12" long
Plastic drop cloth and plastic food wrap

Disposable cups
Kitchen sponge
Water-soluble glue stick
Salt
Spray bottle of water (mister)
Textile pigment (paint)
    Seta Color by Pebeo (French)
    Versatex by Siphon Art (U.S.A.)

TECHNIQUES

RESIST a method of drawing a line to separate colors or to prevent dye from penetrating the fabric.

Commonly used resists are wax (batik), starch paste, or gutta. I have used a water-soluble gutta or, for a quicker method, a water-soluble glue stick. This method does not give as distinct a line as wax, paste or gutta but affords an interesting surface design.

Cover the table with a plastic drop cloth, or use plastic food wrap to cover a smaller area. Draw design lines on the fabric with a glue stick and allow them to dry. Paint the colors onto the fabric and let the paint dry. Heat-set the paint by ironing. Use a press cloth to protect the iron from the resist. Wash the fabric in soap and water to remove the resist, then iron it dry.

BRUSHES for a more painterly effect

Use a 4"-wide inexpensive brush with thin bristles (*not* a ¾"-thick housepainting brush!). Cover the table with plastic. Pour diluted paint into a pie tin and brush on color, using bold, broad strokes. Try various size brushes for a personal effect. Let the fabric dry on the plastic, then heat-set the color when dry.

SPONGE STAMPING for a repeated design

Pour small amounts of full-strength textile paints into the pie tin. Cut shapes such as squares, circles, etc. out of a disposable kitchen sponge. Moisten a piece of sponge and squeeze out the excess water. Cover the table with plastic. Lightly press the sponge into some paint in the pie tin, mixing colors directly on the sponge. Stamp an image onto the fabric. Dip the sponge lightly in water and stamp again. This will mute both the color and the clarity of the image. Restamp with other colors. Let the fabric dry and heat-set with an iron.

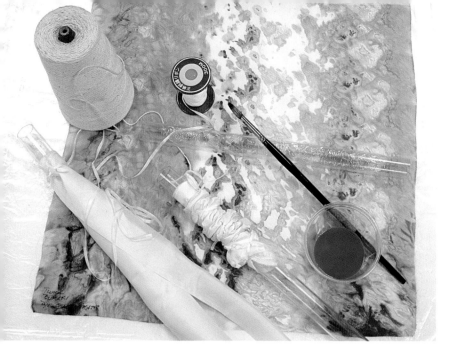

TUBE TIE for a random light-to-dark-value pattern

The tube can be plastic plumbing pipe or a clear acrylic tube. Cover the tube with plastic food wrap to eliminate the static cling of silk. Loosely roll an 18″ by 18″ piece of silk onto the 1″ diameter tube. Tie a string or ribbon at one edge of the tube, securing the rolled silk. Twist the silk on the tube and force the silk up to the tied end. Twist and force the silk up until it measures only about 5″. Secure the silk on the tube with string or ribbon. Apply paint to the surface with a #6 artist's brush. Let the paint dry for about 20 minutes and clip the securing tie. Pull the silk off the tube and let it dry. Iron to heat-set the color. If necessary, spray the fabric with water after heat-setting and iron again to remove wrinkles.

WATERCOLOR for an overall coloration

Dilute paints with water in small containers. Cover the table with a plastic drop cloth. Submerge the silk in water and squeeze out the excess. Arrange the wet silk on the plastic. Wrinkles in the fabric will not affect the final result. With a 1″ paint brush, paint directly on the wet silk with broad, sweeping brush strokes. Use the dilute paint from the container, or mix colors together in another container to obtain additional colors. Be sure to color the whole surface, adding more water and paint as needed. Allow the fabric to dry on the plastic. A pale, random pattern will form on the silk, caused by pooling of the paint on the plastic. This pattern is unpredictable and gives a nice, subtle effect. Iron the fabric when dry to heat-set the paint. Moisten the fabric after heat-setting and re-iron to remove wrinkles.

Three other methods you can try with the above technique also give interesting effects.

1. Sprinkle rock or table salt on the wet, painted fabric. Salt will make an additional fine surface design. A difficulty arises, though, with heat-setting the fabric: you must iron the fabric *before* washing out the salt. Rub excess salt off the fabric and heat-set with an iron, wash to remove the salt, and then re-iron.

2. Mist the painted fabric with a spray bottle of water to add more moisture to the surface. Using a dry piece of fabric, make a print off the first piece by placing the second fabric on top of the first. Remove the second piece after just a minute or two and lay it flat to dry. Iron both pieces when dry to heat-set.

3. Remove the wet, painted fabric from the plastic before the fabric dries. Use a press cloth on the ironing board and a press cloth on the silk, and iron it dry. About 50% of the color will be transferred to the press cloth. This technique makes a very pale painted fabric. Some paint will still be present on the plastic drop cloth and forms small droplets of color. Replace the ironed, dry fabric on the plastic and pick up the droplets of color. This will make a random polka-dot pattern on the fabric. Allow it to dry completely on the plastic and heat-set again.

AN EASY APPROACH
TO FABRIC PIECING

The two basic decisions I make are: the size of the project—a small one such as a vest, or a large one such as a quilt; the choice of a dominant color and the harmonizing colors. My personal approach to designing is to use strip piecing rather than repetitive formal blocks. I know that I am going to make a quilt or a certain garment, and I know approximately how much fabric I will need. I assemble all the fabrics I want to use in my project. I stack the colors in order, either from light to dark or in a comfortable color flow (such as reds through purple, or blues to green). By stacking the colors with just an edge showing, I can see what they will look like in the strip piecing. If the stack of colors is not satisfying, I can now make a decision: I rearrange the grouping of colors and eliminate or add until I have a pleasing combination.

Basically, I use strip-piecing techniques. For beginners, I recommend *The Quick Quiltmaking Handbook* by Barbara Johannah. I use strips which can be manipulated into nine-patch blocks or log-cabin blocks, prairie points and blocks made from pairs of triangles to design most of my work.

When making a garment, I usually choose one of my patterns from *Pieced Clothing* or *Pieced Clothing Variations*. Please refer to these books for specific garment patterns and construction techniques.

Let us assume that we will begin assembling patchwork for a vest. First, I cut the pattern shapes out of underlining such as batting, cotton flannelette or muslin. The patchwork sections will be sewn to these shapes.

To begin strip piecing, I use an OLFA cutter and mat, and plastic templates to cut fabric into strips. The strips are cut 45" long (from selvage to selvage), so every strip

will be approximately the same length. If necessary, shorter lengths can be pieced to make 45″. The strips are cut in different widths so I have a selection from 1″ to 2½″ wide. The strips are arranged in various combinations of color and widths, and these are sewn together in units of 2 or 3 to 5 or 6 colors.

The sewn units of striped colors can now be cut crosswise, such as 2″ wide, into narrow bands of color and assembled together end to end to make a long 2″-wide strip of pieced fabric. Or the sewn units of striped colors can be used as a single large area of color.

After sewing and cutting various units, I begin piecing on the vest shapes. I sew these pieced or single strips of fabric directly through the underlining. This process of sewing patchwork to the underlining secures the layers together. It is appropriate to add a lining to the vest after the patchwork is complete, in order to conceal the stitching lines. Then each garment is finished like a quilt, with binding on all the raw edges.

When making a quilt, I am rather unorthodox: I assemble the fabrics, make the strips and immediately begin sewing the quilt top. I do not sew to an underlining. The top is pieced to the desired size, then batted, backed, quilted, and the edges bound.

TOOLS AND SUPPLIES

OLFA cutter and mat
Plastic templates for strips—1" to 3½" wide
Sewing machine

Cotton fabrics
Batting or underlining
    (cotton flannelette or muslin)

LIST OF COLOR PLATES

All measurements are in inches, and width precedes length.

Page

10   Detail of *Paper Kimono*, kimono shape.

17   **Bonjour Pinkette**

18   Detail of *Takoage*, quilt.

19   Detail of *Chop Suey*, little jacket.

20   Detail of *Razzle Dazzle*, quilt.

21   Detail of *China Doll*, vest.

22   Detail of *Diamonds on Ice*, hand-painted silk kimono.

23   Detail of *Michael's Jacket*, hand-painted Japanese jacket.

24   Detail of *Calligraphy Jacket*, jacket.

25   Detail of *Autumn Leaves*, dyed silk vest.

26   Detail of *When All the Colors Come Dancing*, kimono.

29   **Lord's Cafe (Corner of Gates Road and Paradise Avenue)**

30   *Pieces and Parts* kimono form: cottons, machine-pieced, hand-quilted, 48 × 60, 1985.

31   *Polka Dot Fantasy* quilt: cottons, machine-pieced, hand-quilted; backing: hand-painted cotton; 65 × 65, 1984.

32   *Ginza* quilt: cottons and metallics, machine-pieced, hand-appliquéd, machine- and hand-quilted, 67 × 67, 1984.

33   Detail of *Ginza*, quilt.

34   (top) *Masquerade* quilt: cottons, machine-pieced, hand-quilted, 64 × 64, 1982.

34   (bottom) Detail of *Masquerade*, quilt.

35   *Pasha on the 10:04* kimono: cottons, machine-pieced; lining: hand-painted cotton; 48 × 63, 1984.

36   *Cool Kimono* kimono: cottons, machine-pieced; lining: hand-painted silk; 48 × 60, 1982.

39   **From the Bazaar**

40   **Caravans**

41   *Memories* coat: cottons, machine-pieced, hand-quilted, 1981.

42   Detail of *Painted Chevron* vest: silk and cotton, machine- and hand-pieced, 1984.

43   Detail of *Nine Patch* vest: cottons, machine- and hand-pieced, 1984.

44   *Midnight Celebration* kimono: cottons, machine-pieced; lining: hand-painted silk; 48 × 60, 1983.

45   *Kaleidoscopically Yours* jacket and skirt (reversible): cottons, machine-pieced, 1982

46   Detail of *Kaleidoscopically Yours*, skirt.

49   **Dear Daughter**

50   Detail of *Firebird*, kimono.

51   *Firebird*, kimono: hand-painted silk, hand-cut 2" diamonds, machine-sewn; lining: hand-painted silk with rhinestones; 48 × 72, 1984.

52   *Firebird*, kimono (inside view).

53   *Diamonds on Ice* kimono: hand-painted silks, hand-cut 2" diamonds, machine-sewn; lining: hand-painted silk, hand-quilted; 48 × 60, 1984.

54   Detail of the lining of *Diamonds on Ice*, kimono.

55   *Diamonds on Ice*, kimono (inside view).

56   (top) *Paper Kimono* kimono shape: hand-painted paper and silk, glued and stitched, 38 × 39, 1985.

56   (bottom) *Fitted Jacket* jacket: silks, hand-painted, machine-pieced; lining: hand-painted silk; 1983.

59   **Premiere at the Barbizon**

60   *Robe for a Dragonrider* kimono: cottons and metallics, machine-pieced, hand-quilted; lining: hand-painted cotton; 48 × 60, 1982.

61   (top) Detail of *Robe for a Dragonrider*, kimono.

61   (bottom) Detail of lining of *Robe for a Dragonrider*, kimono.

62   *Metallic Jacket* jacket: metallic and hand-painted silks, machine-pieced, 1983.

64   *Electric Kimono* kimono: metallic and cotton, machine-pieced; lining: hand-painted cotton; 48 × 60, 1983.

65   Model wearing *Opulence* Tibetan vest and kimono: cotton, metallic, and nylon, hand-painted cotton, hand-quilted with sequins, 1985.

66 (left and top) Model wearing *Opulence*, Tibetan vest and kimono.

66 (bottom) Detail of *Opulence*, vest.

69 **Three Beauties: Snow, Moon & Flower**

70 **In the Shadow of My Heart**

71 *Streamers in the Sky* quilt: hand-painted silk, machine- and hand-pieced, hand-quilted, 24 × 18, 1985.

72 Detail of *Spring's Early Dawn*, kimono form.

73 *Spring's Early Dawn* kimono form: hand-painted silks, machine-pieced, hand-quilted, 60 × 60, 1984.

74 (top) *Magenta Triangles* haori coat: hand-painted silks, machine-pieced, hand-quilted, 48 × 36, 1984.

74 (bottom) *Tiffany* quilt: hand-painted silks and cotton, machine-pieced, hand-appliquéd, hand-quilted, 44 × 60, 1984.

75 *In Autumn the Evening Shows Its Lavender* quilt: hand-painted silks, machine- and hand-pieced, hand-appliquéd, hand-quilted, 58 × 58, 1985. (Collection of Suzanna Silverstein)

76 (inset) *Secret Friends with Green* kimono: hand-painted silks, hand-appliquéd, tied, 48 × 50, 1984.

76 Detail of *Secret Friends with Green*, kimono.

77 Detail of *Sundancer 684*, quilt.

78 (left) Detail of *Sundancer 684*, quilt.

78 *Sundancer 684* quilt: hand-painted silks and cottons, hand-appliquéd, machine- and hand-pieced, hand-quilted, 62 × 58, 1984.

81 **Always Chasing Rainbows**

82 Detail of *Night Rainbow*, vest.

83 Detail of *Homage to a Rainbowmaker*, quilt.

84 *Homage to a Rainbowmaker* quilt: cottons, machine-pieced, hand-quilted, 65 × 65, 1983.

85 (bottom) *Starcatcher's Rainbow* skirt, blouse, jacket, and stole: cottons and metallics, machine-pieced, machine-quilted; lining: hand-painted silk; 1983.

85 (top) Detail of *Starcatcher's Rainbow*, stole.

86 *Eric's Quilt* quilt: cottons, machine-pieced, hand-quilted; backing: hand-painted cotton; 45 × 60, 1985.

87 (top) Stole for *Starcatcher's Rainbow*.

87 (right) Detail of *When All the Colors Come Dancing*, kimono.

88 Detail of *When All the Colors Come Dancing*, kimono.

89 *When All the Colors Come Dancing* kimono: cottons and metallics, machine-pieced, hand-quilted, hand-appliquéd; lining: hand-painted silk; 48 × 72, 1983.

90 *Over the Rainbow* coat: cotton, machine-pieced, 1981.

93 **"Ah, Red"**

94 *Red Jacket and Vest* jacket and vest: cottons, machine-pieced, 1983.

95 Detail of *Red Jacket and Vest*, jacket.

96 *Carro* quilt: cottons, machine-pieced, hand-tied and quilted; backing: hand-painted cottons; 46 × 46, 1984.

97 (top) *Hot Kimono* kimono: cottons and metallics, machine-pieced, hand-quilted; lining: hand-painted silk; 48 × 60, 1982.

97 (bottom) Detail of *Hot Kimono*, kimono.

98 *Red Kimono* kimono: cottons, machine-pieced, hand-quilted, 48 × 60, 1981.

99 *Red Kimono*, kimono.

100 *Red Coat* coat: cottons, machine-pieced, 1982.

101 Detail of *Red Coat*, coat.

102 Detail of *Over the Rainbow*, coat.

BIBLIOGRAPHY

Aiken, Joyce, and Jean Ray Laury. *Creating Body Coverings*. New York: Van Nostrand Reinhold, 1973.

Birren, Faber. *Principles of Color*. New York: Van Nostrand Reinhold, 1969.

Bruhn, Wolfgang, and Max Tilke. *A Pictorial History of Costume*. New York: Hastings House, 1973.

Danly, Robert Lyons. *In the Shade of Spring Leaves*. New Haven: Yale University Press, 1981.

DeOsma, Guillermo. *Mariano Fortuny: His Life and Work*. New York: Rizzoli, 1980.

Designer's Guide to Color 2. Introductory essay by James Stockton. San Francisco: Chronicle Books, 1984. (Based on *Haishoku Jiten* by Ikuyoshi Shibukawa and Yumi Takahashi.)

Friedman, Martin. *Hockney Paints the Stage*. New York: Abbeville Press, 1983.

Goethe, Johann Wolfgang von. *Theory of Colours*. Trans. Charles Lock Eastlake. Cambridge, Mass.: The M.I.T. Press, 1973. (Reprint of 1840 London edition.)

Golynets, Sergei. *Ivan Bilibin*. Trans. Glenys Ann Kozlov. New York: Harry N. Abrams, Inc., 1982.

Gouma-Peterson, Thalia. *Miriam Schapiro: A Retrospective 1953-1980*. Wooster, Ohio: College of Wooster, 1980.

Gutcheon, Beth. *The Perfect Patchwork Primer*. New York: Penguin Books, 1973.

Itten, Johannes. *The Elements of Color*. New York: Van Nostrand Reinhold, 1970.

James, Michael. *The Quiltmaker's Handbook*. Englewood Cliffs, N.J.: Prentice-Hall, Inc., 1978.

Japan Style. New York and San Francisco: Kodansha International Ltd., 1980.

Johannah, Barbara. *The Quick Quiltmaking Handbook*. Menlo Park, Cal.: Pride of the Forest Press, 1979.

Klika, Thom. *Rainbows*. New York: St. Martin's Press, 1979.

Klika, Thom. *10,000 Rainbows*. New York: St. Martin's Press, 1983.

Kubota, Itchiku. *Opulence: The Kimonos and Robes of Itchiku Kubota*. New York and San Francisco: Kodansha International Ltd., 1984.

Kueppers, Harald. *Color Atlas*. Trans. Roger Marcinik. Woodbury, N.Y.: Barron's, 1982.

Link, Howard A. *Japanese Genre Paintings from the Kyusei Atami Art Museum*. Tokyo: Benrido, 1980.

Lubell, Cecil. *Textile Collections of the World, Vol. I, II, III*. New York: Van Nostrand Reinhold, 1976, 1977.

McMorris, Penny. *Crazy Quilts*. New York: E. P. Dutton, Inc., 1984.

Noma, Seiroku. *Japanese Costume and Textile Arts*. Trans. Armins Nikovskis. New York: John Weatherhill, Inc., and Tokyo: Heibonsha, 1974. Volume 16 of *The Heibonsha Survey of Japanese Art*.

Prideaux, Tom. *The World of Delacroix 1798-1863*. New York: Time-Life Books, 1966.

Proctor, Richard M., and Jennifer F. Lew. *Surface Design for Fabric*. Seattle: University of Washington Press, 1984.

Rhodes, Zandra. *The Art of Zandra Rhodes*. Boston: Houghton Mifflin Co., 1985.

Sargent, Walter. *The Enjoyment and Use of Color*. New York: Dover Publications, Inc., 1964.

Shikibu, Murasaki. *The Tale of Genji*. Trans. Edward G. Seidensticker. New York: Alfred A. Knopf, 1976.

Spencer, Charles. *Leon Bakst*. New York: Rizzoli, 1973.

Tanaka, Ikko, and Kazuko Koike, eds. *Japan Design: The Four Seasons in Design*. San Francisco: Chronicle Books, 1984.

Tanaka, Ikko, and Kazuko Koike, eds. *Japanese Coloring*. Tokyo: Libro Port Co., Ltd., 1982.

The Spirit of Colors: The Art of Karl Gerstner. Ed. Henri Stierlin, trans. Dennis Q. Stephenson. Cambridge, Mass.: The M.I.T. Press, 1981.

Tilke, Max. *Costume Patterns and Designs*. New York: Hastings House, 1974.

Truitt, Anne. *Daybook*. New York: Penguin Books, 1984.

Vreeland, Diana. *D.V.* New York: Vintage Books, 1985.

Wichmann, Siegfried. *Japonisme: The Japanese Influence on Western Art in the 19th and 20th Centuries*. New York: Harmony Books, 1981.

Wilkin, Karen. *Frankenthaler: Works on Paper 1949-1984*. New York: George Braziller, 1984.

SOURCE LIST

Artists' Medium
P.O. Box 414
Williston, VT 05495
pigment

Cerulean Blue, Ltd.
P.O. Box 21168
Seattle, WA 98111
dyes, pigments, fabrics

Color Craft
P.O. Box 936
Avon, CT 06001
dyes, pigments

Fab Dec
3553 Old Post Rd.
San Angelo, TX 76904
dyes, pigments, fabrics

Pro Chemical & Dye Inc.
P.O. Box 14
Somerset, MA 02726
dyes

Savoir-Faire
3020 Bridgeway, Suite 305
Sausalito, CA 94965
dye

Siphon Art
74 Hamilton Dr.
Ignacio, CA 94947
pigment (Versatex)

Sureway Trading Enterprises
826 Pine Ave., Suites 5 & 6
Niagara Falls, NY 14301
silk fabrics, dye

Testfabrics
P.O. Drawer "O"
Middlesex, NJ 08846
fabrics

Textile Artists' Supply
3006 San Pablo Ave.
Berkeley, CA 94702
dyes, pigments

Thai Silks
252 State St.
Los Altos, CA 94022
silk fabrics

I enjoy quilting and patchwork and it has become for me a contemporary art form and full-time occupation. The work included in this book is representative of most of the quilts and garments I have made in the past six years. I have chosen to share with you what I consider the best and most innovative work.